3/19

Freedom

Amanda Rondeau

Consulting Editor
Monica Marx, M.A./Reading Specialist

Published by SandCastle™, an imprint of ABDO Publishing Company, 4940 Viking Drive, Edina, Minnesota 55435.

Printed in the United States.

Credits
Edited by: Pam Price
Curriculum Coordinator: Nancy Tuminelly
Cover and Interior Design and Production: Mighty Media
Photo Credits: Corbis Images, Comstock, Digital Vision, Eyewire Images, PhotoDisc

Library of Congress Cataloging-in-Publication Data
Rondeau, Amanda, 1974-
    Freedom / Amanda Rondeau.
       p. cm. -- (United we stand)
    Includes index.
    Summary: Describes the many kinds of freedom we have in the United States, including the freedom to vote, freedom of religion, and freedom of speech.
    ISBN 1-57765-878-7
    1. Civil rights--United States--Juvenile literature. 2. Liberty--Juvenile literature. [1. Civil rights. 2. Freedom.] I. Title. II. Series.

JC599.U5 R612 2002
323.44'0973--dc21
                                                                  2002066404

SandCastle™ books are created by a professional team of educators, reading specialists, and content developers around five essential components that include phonemic awareness, phonics, vocabulary, text comprehension, and fluency. All books are written, reviewed, and leveled for guided reading, early intervention reading, and Accelerated Reader® programs and designed for use in shared, guided, and independent reading and writing activities to support a balanced approach to literacy instruction.

Let Us Know

After reading the book, SandCastle would like you to tell us your stories about reading. What is your favorite page? Was there something hard that you needed help with? Share the ups and downs of learning to read. We want to hear from you! To get posted on the ABDO Publishing Company Web site, send us email at:

sandcastle@abdopub.com

SandCastle Level: Transitional

What is freedom?

Freedom is the right to make choices about our lives.

Martin Luther King, Jr., wanted freedom for everyone.

People in the United States have the freedom to do many things.

Freedom is part of our lives.

We have the freedom to vote after we turn 18.

Voters choose who our leaders will be.

We have the freedom of religion.

We have the right to believe in any religion.

We have the freedom to choose where we live.

You might choose the city.

We have freedom of speech.

We have the right to our own ideas and to tell people what we think.

We also have the freedom to go to school.

We can learn about many things.

This helps us to become what we want to be when we grow up.

Freedom is an important part of our country.

It allows us to make choices about our own lives.

The bald eagle is our national bird.

What does it stand for?

(freedom)

Index

Glossary

choice	the chance to choose someone or something
ideas	thoughts, opinions, beliefs, or plans
national	something of or related to a nation as a whole
religion	belief in and worship of a God or ~~gods~~
vote	to make a choice in an election or other type of poll

About SandCastle™

A professional team of educators, reading specialists, and content developers created the SandCastle™ series to support young readers as they develop reading skills and strategies and increase their general knowledge. The SandCastle™ series has four levels that correspond to early literacy development in young children. The levels are provided to help teachers and parents select the appropriate books for young readers.

Emerging Readers
(no flags)

Beginning Readers
(1 flag)

Transitional Readers
(2 flags)

Fluent Readers
(3 flags)

These levels are meant only as a guide. All levels are subject to change.

ABDO
Publishing Company

To see a complete list of SandCastle™ books and other nonfiction titles from ABDO Publishing Company, visit **www.abdopub.com** or contact us at:

4940 Viking Drive, Edina, Minnesota 55435 • 1-800-800-1312 • fax: 1-952-831-1632